How to Safely Replace Your Day Job

An Insider's Guide to Making Money with Affiliate Marketing

Don Loyd

Don Loyd

How to Safely Replace Your Day Job
An Insider's Guide to Making Money with Affiliate Marketing

© 2017 Don Loyd
All Rights Reserved

DreamMaker Press, LLC
Denver, Colorado

First Printing

Team Work Makes the Dream Work

Books by DreamMaker Press

Creating Wealth for Women
Creating Wealth in Declining Real Estate Markets
Creating Wealth Manual
The Cure for Declining Income
Move in Now – Buy Later
Taking Back Your Life
How to Use a Buy/Sell Analysis
I Can Be an Author
Creative Real Estate Your Way to Riches
The Right Real Estate Exit Strategy
How to Buy Your First Home
Developing Attitudes for Life Change
How to Improve Your Credit Rating
Living the Dream
A Practical Guide for the FSBO
Mortgage Magic
Retirement Recovery Guide
The Business of Real Estate Investing
The Six Figure Real Estate Broker
The Secret to 7 Figures

Disclaimer

The contents, discussions, legal and financial information and other materials contained in this book are for informational or educational purposes only and no content should be construed as, or relied upon as, legal, financial or investment advice; as the providing of legal, financial or investment services or as the recommendation of forms or of the opinions from author.

Table of Contents

Introduction 5

Chapter 1
Finding Affiliate Programs 10

Chapter 2
Finding Affiliate Programs 14

Chapter 3
Outselling Other Affiliates 16

Chapter 4
The ClickBank Advantage 25

Chapter 5
Checklist 30

Chapter 6
Welcome to The Start of a
      Life With New Possibilities 36

Introduction

Affiliate marketing has always been one of the most popular methods of making money.

For anyone who is just starting out, there's no easier or faster method of generating income. For anyone who already operates their own online business, selling other people's products can create a substantial boost to the income they're already receiving.

The primary appeal comes from the fact that the only task the affiliate has to perform is promote whatever product or service they believe has substantial sales potential. The owner of the product or service does everything else.

In theory, you don't even need a website in order to make money as an affiliate. You can simply promote your assigned affiliate link and then send prospective buyers to the owner's sales page.

Of course, the obvious drawback is that almost every other affiliate will be doing the exact same thing. If all you're doing is directing targeted traffic through your affiliate sales link, you'll be competing on an equal level with countless other people who are promoting the same product.

The only way to break out of the pack is to market and promote the affiliate product in a more intelligent and aggressive manner.

Those who are referred to as "super" affiliates, make a great deal of money selling other people's products. That's because they market and promote them in the same way they would their own products.

Even though there's a sales page associated with each of the affiliate products, they create a page on their own website. The purpose of that page is to pre-sell the item. In other words, they get the prospect primed and ready to purchase prior to sending them to the owner's sales site.

They also use pay per click advertising to gain targeted prospects. They know that in order to make money, they have to spend money.

Of course, most of them have become masters of pay per click. They know exactly what works, exactly how much to bid, and exactly how to attract the right prospects.

And because they've learned how to play the game so well, they most often generate a great deal more money than if they had simply used free advertising methods.

But pay per click and using their own website to promote products are only two of the methods they use. Others include...

- ✓ Writing product reviews and personal endorsements, recommendations, and testimonials.

- ✓ Operating niche blogs that are directly associated with the products they're promoting.

- ✓ Writing and distributing articles that contain information that's related to individual products (which includes their affiliate link).

- ✓ Offering a special bonus that is only available if the product is purchased through the affiliate's own sales link.

- ✓ Giving away free tips and information, either on their website or distributed through ebooks or autoresponder messages.

- ✓ Capturing prospects names and email addresses for future contact and ongoing follow-up.

- ✓ Using their own marketing and promotional materials.

Although each of those methods are both valuable and effective, the last one is extremely important.

While every other affiliate is simply copying and pasting solo ads that the owner of the product has made available, the super affiliate is developing their own unique and original sales content.

Instead of delivering the same old message every other affiliate is handing out, they can put their own personal spin on it. That means they can make the offer seem more valuable, more appealing, and more original. And of course, they will ultimately generate more sales.

But that's not all they do…

They also ensure their success by making certain they're off to the right start. Rather than jump on every program, product, and service that comes their way, they carefully pick and choose ones they're confident can be marketed and promoted effectively.

Although a certain degree of instinct and past experience works well in that regard, there are basic factors which will help anyone choose the best products. Things like…

- ✓ determining the level of interest and demand

- ✓ evaluating whether or not the sales page is capable of converting the prospects you send there into buyers

- ✓ verifying the overall quality and value of the product

✓ having sufficient information about the product to market it effectively

Super affiliates don't gain their status overnight. They work hard at what they do and put in whatever time and effort is necessary in order to outsell everyone else in their affiliate arena.

And the ultimate payoff? A substantial income that be generated over and over again, month after month and year after year, for as long as they wish to continue marketing and promoting affiliate products.

1.
How to Choose the Right Products

When you consider all the products and programs that are capable of generating affiliate income, it can be mighty difficult choosing which ones have the most potential.

In most instances, you won't know for certain until you actually start promoting any given product. But there are factors that can help diminish the risk of choosing products that have little or no potential.

1. First and foremost, you need to establish whether or not there's even a viable demand for a product. Aside from determining if people want the product, you have to find out what type of people would be interested and if you can easily reach that target audience.

2. How good is the product sales page? If it doesn't look as though it can convert visitors into buyers, you have to decide how much work it will take on your part to override that particular drawback. Then you need to decide if it's worth the extra effort you'll invest.

Overall, you have to decide whether the website will help or hinder your ability to make sales. Go with your instincts. If you don't feel comfortable with the look, the sales copy, or the order process, chances are the average viewer won't either.

3. Can you make enough profit by promoting the product? Some owners reward their affiliates by giving them generous commissions while others merely offer a very small percentage. For the most part, those differences are associated with two very specific categories... digital and physical products.

For example, you can usually make at least 50% commission selling ebooks and software products. With physical items such as vitamins, print books, and pet products, an affiliate commission can be relatively low (on average, somewhere between 5% and 10%).

Although the percentage is important, it also depends on the price of the product. If you're selling an exercise machine that retails for $1800, even a minimal 10% commission will gain you $180 for each sale that you make.

On the other hand, if you're an affiliate for Amazon (http://www.amazon.com), you'll be dealing with items that most often carry a very low sales price. In order to gain any substantial level of income, you'll need to move an incredibly large volume of products.

4. The quality of the product is extremely important. If you yourself don't feel confident about how good it is or how well it performs, it's going to be

difficult for you to launch a successful promotional campaign, much less maintain it over an extended period of time.

5. You need to have the ability to track and monitor everything related to your affiliate activities. That would include things like the number of visitors you send to each sales page, how many of them actually made a purchase, and running sales and refund statistics.

Make certain that you can do that, either through the program or using your own independent tracking device. This will keep you abreast of each product's performance, allowing you to determine which campaigns need to be tweaked, increased, or dropped altogether.

2.
Finding Affiliate Programs

There are three basic methods for locating good affiliate programs...

1. Conduct searches based on a particular niche market.

2. Sign up to use the services of an affiliate marketing network.

3. Search through the categories of affiliate program directories.

The first option will require a considerable amount of time, but it's definitely worth the effort. Assuming, of course, you've completed all the necessary preliminary work which would guarantee a positive outcome.

That would include things like determining your exact target audience, choosing specific and highly relevant keywords, and establishing what criteria would constitute a fair and equitable affiliate program.

The search itself would be conducted in two stages...

The first stage would involve the keywords. You would first need to select a list of search phrases that are highly relevant to the product. Then you would conduct searches using each of those keywords. This will lead you to niche markets and their products.

The second stage would involve any given keyword plus the word affiliate. For example, "dog training affiliate" or "affiliate dog training". What this will generally turn up is either an affiliate program for products that are associated with that particular keyword or a content site that is already an affiliate.

Either way, it allows for further action with regard to becoming an affiliate for a specific keyword or product niche.

With the second option, you simply open a main account with the affiliate network which in turn entitles you to promote any of the products that are included within their listings.

Although these affiliate networks might not always be as capable of giving you exact matches to what you're looking for, they can be incredible time savers.

Affiliate marketing websites like Commission Junction (http://www.cj.com) and Click Bank (http://www.clickbank.com) make it extremely easy to locate good affiliate programs. And generally, for products and services that are highly compatible with the niche or target audience you'll be reaching.

Be aware, however, that only Commission Junction offers all ranges of products, services, and programs - both digital and tangible.

ClickBank, on the other hand, only handles digital products such as ebooks and software programs. If it can't be downloaded or delivered electronically, you won't find it in the ClickBank Marketplace (http://marketplace.clickbank.net).

The third option allows you to search for affiliate programs by category, just like you can with networks such as Commission Junction and ClickBank. The only difference is, you'll be signing up for any of the programs you choose independently (through the product owner's affiliate process). All the directory does is provide a convenient method for locating affiliate programs. The rest is up to you.

Here are several popular affiliate directories...

Associate Programs
http://www.associateprograms.com

Affiliate Match
http://www.affiliatematch.com

Affiliates Directory
http://www.affiliatesdirectory.com

Affiliate Programs Directory
http://www.affiliate-programs-directory.com

If you need more resources, simply conduct a search using the term "affiliate program directory".

3.
Outselling Other Affiliates

Having to compete with hundreds or even thousands of other affiliates can make the task of generating income extremely difficult. And the only way to combat all that competition is to come up with methods and techniques that will make you stand out from the crowd.

Here are several ways you can do that...

1. Use Your Own Website

If you don't already have a website, get one. If you have a website but it doesn't lend itself to promoting other people's products and services, put a site together that does.

Although you can promote affiliate products without a website, there are distinct advantages to having a home base.

The most important advantage is the fact that you can pre-sell the products. Rather than send cold prospects to the owner's sales page, you'll have them warmed up and ready to make the purchase.

How you warm them up depends on the product itself. With some of them you can simply write a positive and glowing testimonial, telling them

How to Safely Replace Your Day Job

just how great the product is and how much benefit you receive whenever you use it.

With other products, you might want to give them a condensed sales pitch that includes a common problem (poor performance on the golf course) and the ultimate solution (a revolutionary new club that is guaranteed to improve their score).

2. Write Personal Reviews And Recommendations

There's a reason TV commercials that have celebrities promoting products are so popular. If so-and-so drinks that soda or wears those jeans or drives that car, they must be worth buying.

Having someone personally endorse a product is the number one sales booster. And even though you might not be a celebrity, your personal recommendation will go a long way in convincing buyers how good your affiliate product is.

Review the product in a positive light. Use information from the owner's sales page or list benefits that you yourself have thought of. Give the prospective buyers a solid reason to click over to the product website.

Implementing the usual sales approach is fine. But the most effective tactic, the one that will quickly and easily increase the conversion rate, is you personally singing the praises of whatever product you're promotin

3. Operate A Niche Blog

There's no better method for promoting products than a blog. Naturally, you can do the same thing in a newsletter, but that only gets read by those individuals who are already on your mailing list.

With a blog, you can reach an unlimited number of people who would be interested in the type of products you're promoting.

Of course, you can't simply use the blog to sell things. You have to provide valuable and useful content, something that will not only make people listen, but will have them returning on a regular basis.

The easiest content - at least for anyone who relies on affiliate sales - is simply to provide product reviews. If, for example, you promote various pet supplies and training ebooks, you could create a blog for that particular niche and then include in-depth reports about different aspects of individual products.

You could also give tips and advice with regard to using any of the products. Or you could provide ideas on how the products can best be utilized. You could even ask readers to offer their own opinions and recommendations.

In most instances, these types of postings will spur comments from viewers, which in turn will spur comments from other viewers. And of course, the more comments that get posted, the more interest will be generated overall.

You can use blog software or you can simply sign up with one of the free online blog services. The most popular one is Blogger, located at http://www.blogger.com.

4. Write Articles

There's no better way to get personal recognition than writing and distributing your own articles. And once you establish recognition, all of your product endorsements will be taken even more seriously.

When it comes to choosing topics for your articles, always pick something that is directly related to at least one of the products you're promoting. That way you can recommend the product and include your affiliate link right there within the article.

And make certain you take full advantage of the author's resource box.

If you have a primary sales website, where you promote affiliate products, include that link. If you have a blog where you review products, include that link as well. Or, if you have a newsletter and would prefer to solicit more subscribers, direct readers to the page that gives them all the necessary publication and signup information.

Once you've written articles, you need to submit them to as many online directories as you can. And always let people know that your articles are free to re-publish as long as no changes are made and the resource box is included.

Here are three of the most popular article directories...

Article City
http://www.articlecity.com

Ezine Articles
http://www.ezinearticles.com

Article Feeder
http://www.articlefeeder.com

5. Offer A Special Bonus

This is by far the best method for outselling other affiliates. Basically, you enhance the owner's original product package by throwing in yet another product (or products) at no extra cost.

Of course, the more valuable and unique the bonus, the higher the possibility of making more sales than the next guy. The only other criteria is that whatever bonus you choose, it needs to be directly related to the main product.

Although you could certainly offer a tangible item, the least troublesome bonus would be something digital. That way, you don't have to worry about physically delivering it to the buyer.

For example, if the product you're selling is that revolutionary new golf club, you could create an ebook that has tips on how a golfer can improve their swing. Or, you could create a video that actually shows them how to do it properly.

The point is, you want a bonus that the buyer can simply download once they've made the initial product purchase. That automatically reduces the amount of work involved in delivering the bonus.

Naturally, the amount of time and money you invest in creating the digital bonus will depend on how much money you receive as an affiliate for each and every sale.

Just keep in mind that you'll only have the cost of creating a digital bonus once. But the value of offering prospective buyers a special bonus could easily bring in substantial income for a considerably long period of time.

And make certain you clearly announce that the bonus can only be acquired if they make their purchase through your affiliate link. If they get the product anywhere else, under any conditions other than yours, they won't receive the bonus you're offering.

6. Give Away Free Tips And Information

Rather than dismiss all those viewers who take a look at your offer but don't purchase right away, you should offer them free tips and information. Naturally, the content will be directly related to the products you're promoting.

You can place that content on your website but you also need to provide methods in which the viewer will have the information available on their own computer.

For example...

- ✓ Put together a downloadable list of frequently asked questions regarding the product and how to use it.

- ✓ Create an ebook that includes ideas for gaining the full potential of a product or service.

- ✓ Develop an autoresponder instruction, how-to, or general information ecourse that will be delivered over a period of subsequent days or weeks.

In each instance that you deliver advice, tips, or information, make certain you also include specific details about the product it's associated with. And of course, you'll need to include your personal affiliate link as well.

7. Capture Names And Email Addresses

One of the major drawbacks of being an affiliate is the fact that you don't generally have an opportunity to gain the names and email addresses of people who purchase through your affiliate link.

Plus, you're going to attract plenty of targeted individuals who just aren't ready to purchase during their first exposure to your offer.

Do whatever it takes to encourage prospects to sign up for your mailing list. If you create an autoresponder ecourse (and use a qualified autoresponder service), you'll automatically receive names and email addresses. But what about any free downloads such as ebooks or reports that you're giving away?

Instead of merely letting viewers take them anonymously, have them fill out and submit a form first. That way, they get the free information, you get their name and email address.

Now you can contact them over an extended period of time, continuing to give them valuable tips and information regarding the product or type of products they were initially interested in.

Just don't abuse the privilege by sending them promotional messages and nothing else.

Your ultimate goal is to sell something but in order to move your mailing list members into a buying position you first need to establish a relationship of trust and respect.

That will be accomplished by supplying them with valuable information while at the same time letting them know the benefits the product will provide.

8. Use Your Own Ads And Promotional Materials

Most affiliates rely on promotional materials that are supplied by the owner of the product. That would include things like solo and classified ads, banners, pre-written sales copy, and cover and product images.

Although it might be quality material, the fact that so many other affiliates will be using it will automatically dilute the impact and effectiveness.

You can get much better results by writing your own ads, writing fresh sales copy, and creating new banners and images. The primary purpose is to have something different than any of the other affiliates. But it's also possible that what you create is superior to the original marketing materials.

Overall, it's simply a matter of doing something different and unique. And doing it better and more aggressively than anyone else.

4.
The ClickBank Advantage

The primary advantage of Click Bank - aside from the fact that's a virtual gold mine for affiliates - is the innate simplicity of using and implementing it.

Once you join Click Bank (for free), you'll have your own personal ID which in turn will be included in any of your product affiliate links.

For example, if your ClickBank ID is "softsell" and the product owner's ID is "eproducts", your affiliate URL address would be...

http://softsell.eproducts.hop.clickbank.net

To find products that fit your niche market or target audience, all you need to do is visit the ClickBank Marketplace (when you first get to the website, click on "Earn Commissions").

The marketplace divides the products into main categories...

Business to Business	Health & Fitness	Home & Family
Computing & Internet	Money & Employment	Marketing & Ads
Fun & Entertainment	Sports & Recreation	Society & Culture

#1 Affiliate Commissions Affiliates EARN 70% per sale. www.NoAdWare.net	Make $500-$3900 Daily! Affiliates EARN $$$ per sale. www.Mp3Musiq.com	Best Anti-Spyware Program Affiliates EARN 65% per sale. www.SpyWareNuker.com
Make $5,000 Weekly Easily! Affiliates EARN 50% per sale. www.3500weekly.com	#1 Detective Affiliate Payouts Affiliates EARN 75% per sale. www.Records-Registry.com	? 15min to $1000+ per week ? Affiliates EARN 75% per sale. www.cdMarketing.com

Clicking on any of those category links will allow you to drill down even farther. For example, if you click on Health & Fitness, you'll receive a list of sub-categories that include Addiction, Fitness, Beauty, Nutrition, Diet, Medicine, and Mental Health.

The first ten listings in each category are the top affiliate earners. This allows you to see at a glance which products are making the most amount of money for their affiliates. But that doesn't mean you should choose any of the top ten.

Sometimes it's much more productive to go with one of the lower listings and then make it a top earner for you personally. For one thing, you won't have as much competition. Secondly, it will force you to get a bit more creative with your marketing and promotion.

Of course, the basic product selection criteria still applies here. With any product you're considering, for example, you still need to click over to their sales page and establish how good it will be in converting prospects to buyers.

Aside from evaluating the sales copy, you also need to make certain that the sales process doesn't sabotage your own efforts. Things like...

- ✓ Allowing people to purchase through alternative methods which would bypass or exclude your ClickBank affiliate link.

- ✓ Selling various non-related products on the same page.

- ✓ Products are being sold on the same page but the link doesn't give credit to your ClickBank affiliate ID.

- ✓ Names and email addresses are being captured by the owner for future follow-up which could rob you of your rightful affiliate commission.

Overall, you want to see a nice clean sales page that is focused on the one ClickBank product you're promoting and nothing else.

If the sales page doesn't do that - and it's diluted with all sorts of other things that benefit the owner but not you - pass on the product and find one that is worth your time and effort.

Once you've chosen the "right" products, you'll need to begin marketing and promotion. And since there's no more effective and profitable method than using pay per click, the perfect money-making combination is ClickBank affiliate products and Google AdWords advertising.

The power of AdWords is undeniable. It allows you the ability to...

- ✓ advertise directly to highly targeted audiences

- ✓ display your ad almost immediately

- ✓ start bringing in money almost immediately

- ✓ link directly to any landing page

- ✓ keep accurate and highly advanced ad statistics

Of course, the success of your AdWords campaigns will be dependent almost entirely on the strength of the keywords you've selected.

Keep in mind that the winning formula is to choose keywords that are widely searched for but have little or no competition. In order to conduct that type of research, you have two choices... invest a great deal of time sorting through all the data, or simply use Ad Word Analyzer (http://www.adwordanalyzer.com).

Right away, you'll have a comprehensive list of all search terms that are related to any keyword you input. You'll also know how many searches were conducted on all of those phrases and how many AdWords campaigns already exist (your competition).

But rather than simply use Ad Word Analyzer to find good keywords, you can also use it to find the best markets. Even before you locate any products. Then, once you've unveiled the most promising campaign possibilities, you can use ClickBank to locate specific items to promote.

Checklist

- ✓ For anyone just starting out, there's no easier or faster method of generating income than affiliate marketing.

- ✓ For anyone who already operates their own online business, selling other people's products can create a substantial boost to their existing income.

- ✓ If all you're doing is directing targeted traffic through your affiliate sales link, you'll be competing on an equal level with countless other people who are promoting the same product.

- ✓ Super affiliates make a great deal of money selling other people's products, mainly because they market and promote them the same as they would their own products.

- ✓ Super affiliates use pay per click as their primary method of advertising (they know they have to spend money in order to make money).

- ✓ While other affiliates are simply copying and pasting ads that the owner of the product has made available, super affiliates are developing their own unique and original sales content.

- ✓ Rather than jump on every program, product, and service that comes their way, super affiliates carefully pick and choose ones they're confident can be marketed and promoted effectively.

- ✓ When choosing a product, you need to establish whether or not there's a viable demand.

- ✓ If you don't feel comfortable with a product's website, sales copy, or order process, chances are the average viewer won't either.

- ✓ If you don't feel confident about the quality of a product, it's going to be difficult for you to launch a successful promotional campaign.

- ✓ You need to have the ability to track and monitor everything related to your affiliate activities.

- ✓ To locate good affiliate programs you can conduct searches based on a particular niche market, sign up to use the services of an affiliate marketing network, or search through the categories of affiliate program directories.

- ✓ Affiliate marketing websites like Commission Junction and ClickBank make it extremely easy to locate good affiliate programs - products that are highly compatible with your niche or target audience.

- ✓ Commission Junction offers all ranges of products, services, and programs - both digital and tangible.

- ✓ ClickBank only handles digital products such as ebooks and software programs.

- ✓ Use your own website to promote and pre-sell your affiliate products.

- ✓ One of the most effective tactics is to write personal product reviews and recommendations.

- ✓ With a niche blog you can reach an unlimited number of people who would be interested in the type of products you're promoting.

- ✓ There's no better way to get personal recognition than writing and distributing your own articles.

- ✓ One of the best methods for outselling other affiliates is to enhance the owner's original product package with yet another product (bonus) at no extra cost.

- ✓ Deliver advice, tips, and information along with specific details about the related product and your affiliate link.

- ✓ Encourage viewers to sign up for your mailing list so you can contact them over an extended period of time, continuing to give them valuable tips and information about the product.

- ✓ You can achieve much better results by writing your own ads, writing fresh sales copy, and creating new banners and images.

- ✓ The primary advantage of ClickBank - aside from the fact that's a virtual gold mine for affiliates - is the innate simplicity of using and implementing it.

- ✓ Since there's no more effective and profitable advertising method than using pay per click, the perfect money-making combination is ClickBank and AdWords.

Resources

Commission Junction
http://www.cj.com

ClickBank
http://www.clickbank.com

ClickBank Marketplace
http://marketplace.clickbank.net

Amazon
http://www.amazon.com

Associate Programs
http://www.associateprograms.com

Affiliate Match
http://www.affiliatematch.com

Affiliates Directory
http://www.affiliatesdirectory.com

Affiliate Programs Directory
http://www.affiliate-programs-directory.com

Blogger

http://www.blogger.com

Article City
http://www.articlecity.com

Ezine Articles
http://www.ezinearticles.com

Article Feeder
http://www.articlefeeder.com

Google AdWords
http://adwords.google.com

Ad Word Analyzer
http://www.adwordanalyzer.com

6.
Welcome to the Start of a Life With New Possibilities.

One of my goals is to make dreamers of people. I want you to see the possibilities available and opportunities you can create. I want you to succeed in business and in your personal life. I want you to feel the exhilaration and rush of success.

Success means different things to different people. For some, it may mean having meaningful relationships. For others, it might mean making enough money so they can quit their day jobs. For still others, it may mean giving away a million dollars every year.

No matter how you personally define success, achieving it boils down to having a vision for tomorrow and a way to get there. The way to get there is through setting goals, creating a definitive plan for achieving those goals, and then taking the necessary action, even when that means leaving your comfort zone and venturing into unfamiliar or uncomfortable territory.

Having the dream and knowing how to achieve it will be meaningless unless you do what you need to do to make it happen. Success means reaching your goals, not simply dreaming about them.

The Greek Philosopher, Epictetus, said, "First say to yourself what you would be, and then do what you have to do."

To help you achieve success, I offer you a list of what I believe are the ten most common reasons people fail to realize their dreams, and advice on how to overcome them.

The Author

1. Get a Clear Vision of What You Want to Accomplish

If you don't know what it is that you want, how will you know when you've arrived? The more distinct your dream becomes, and the better you articulate it, the faster you'll achieve it.

I want you to try an experiment. Put your feet flat on the floor with your back straight. Now, relax and close your eyes. I want you to picture success, whatever that is to you. I want you to explore the benefits and pleasure of that success. I want you to feel the exhilaration. Taste it, smell it.

Success, however you viewed it in your dream, is true: it's your reality. That reality can be extended and enlarged upon. But without *seeing* what you now understand success to be, you'll never know what it is. In my book, **My New Reality Journal**, I encourage you to dream.

I want you to have huge, expansive dreams.

And I want you to clearly see where it is you're going.

2. Deal With the Fear of Failure

Many people never really try to succeed because they fear failure. I'll let you in
on a secret: it's okay to fail. In fact, I give you my permission to fail.

I've learned some of my most important lessons through failure. It is true that some fear is healthy. It is crucial to remember, however, to keep your fears and worries in perspective: if you let them overwhelm you, they may rob you of your dreams.

Successful entrepreneurs refuse to let worry, fear and uncertainty hold them back from reaching their goals and realizing their potential. I want the same for you.

I challenge you to eliminate from your vocabulary words like *if, can't, never, won't,* etc.

Don't say, *"If I'd had a better childhood, I could've ____"* or, *"I can't ____. I'm not smart or good looking enough."*

> Don't think things like:
> *"I'm such a jerk. How could I have said that?"*
> *"I'm a loser. I'll never get anywhere."*
> *"I'm so stupid. I should have learned this by now."*
> *"I don't fit in. I don't belong with these people."*
> *"I'll never be good enough. I'll never do it right."*
> *"I'm permanently emotionally damaged. I'll never be okay."*
> *"No one could love me. I'm not lovable."*

Those kinds of words, and that kind of thinking, will almost certainly become self-fulfilling prophecies that will take you down a path away from where you want to go. Replace them with positive affirmations – restated in terms that reinforce positive behavior and a positive mindset.

Try these:

"This is going to be hard, but I know I can do it."

"I am as capable as anyone else."

"I have my own special talents and abilities."

"I'll stick with this as long as it takes."

"I'm a great person!"

These positive affirmations, especially when spoken frequently, will result in a new reality. You will see yourself in a new light. Just remember: whatever you think about yourself as it relates to success and achieving your dreams is true.

3. Possess Determination

We all face challenges that test our resolve. Often a challenge will stop us dead in our tracks. We hit a roadblock and our forward motion ceases. The goal, then, is to face such challenges without reservation and turn them into opportunities so we can continue forward.

Challenges can be viewed as an exciting ride. They can turn life into a treasure hunt or a grand adventure because you never know what you're going to find tomorrow.

If I come up against a brick wall, I try to find the crack in the mortar or a hidden door I can open that will enable me to press on. Sometimes I have to go around the wall, and that's okay, too. It's still a journey worth taking.

I used to pray for challenges. I loved the opportunity to do what "they" said couldn't be done. If someone told me I couldn't, I had to prove him or her wrong. It was like saying to a dog, "sic 'em." I would charge out and do the undoable.

Determination is one thing that separates those who succeed from those who don't. Once you have a vision of where you want to go, resolve – *firmly* - to get there.

4. Make a Plan of Action

To achieve a level of success, and hopefully significance, you need to create a precise plan detailing exactly what you must do in order to realize your dream. If you don't write it down, how will know you know if you are making progress toward the goal? Be sure, too, to set a timetable for the completion of your tasks. Open-ended tasks seem always to be pushed to the rear of the priorities.

Break your objectives into daily activities and then manage those activities. You'll be surprised at how easy it is to complete a lot of work when you manage your time well. Don't let the phone, walk-in customers or whatever "emergencies" may present themselves rule your life. Take charge.

During certain hours, I refuse to take phone calls. I let them go to voice mail and return them when I arrive at the allotted time. I used to have a script on my voice mail that said, "Thanks for calling. I have several appointments today. I can return your call between 10 and 11 A.M. or 3 and 4 P.M. Please let me know when the best time for you would be." That simple script gave me back my life.

When you write your strategy, post it where you can easily see it and read it. You'll find that the more you look at it, the more likely you will be to accomplish the tasks you've set for yourself.

Also, I find that it helps to deal with difficult things first: get anything distasteful or disagreeable over with as soon as you can, so you can enjoy the rest of the day. Also, do all you can without putting things off. Thomas Carlyle, the 9th Century Scottish essayist, wrote: "Men do less than they ought, unless they do all they can."

4. Make Adjustments

You will have to make adjustments in your life to focus on reaching the success you want. In order to make the time you will need, you may have to cut back on or even give up certain activities. The trick is to prioritize. You don't have to skip your daughter's basketball game or leave the bowling league or Friday night poker. But almost everyone has something he or she can spend less time on. Do you *have* to do the crossword or Sudoku *every* day? Try spending less time watching TV, manicuring the lawn, visiting friends on *Facebook*.

Are you surrounded by people who can help you succeed? People can be a great help to you in reaching your goal, but they can also be a hindrance. Don't feel pressured by the friend who tells you not to worry about it, that you can do it tomorrow. Let people know that you are available only after you've done the things you need to do.

5. Eliminate Negative Thinking

Everyone has some self-doubt. However, these two questions will help you. Ask yourself everyday:

    1. Did I give my best effort to today's activities?
    2. Did I move closer to reaching my goals?

The answer to both, of course, should be "yes." If it isn't, though, don't kick yourself. Ask yourself why not, and do things differently tomorrow. Remember the positive affirmations mentioned earlier.

Once again, it is important to look at the people in your life. You'll find it easier to do the things you need to do if people support your goals and respect your needs.

> A positive person anticipates happiness, health and success, and believes he or she can overcome any obstacle and difficulty.
>
> Positive thinking is not accepted by everyone. Some, consider it as nonsense, and scoff at people who follow it, but there is a growing number of people, who accept positive thinking as a fact, and believe in its effectiveness.
>
> It seems that this subject is gaining popularity, as evidenced by the many books, lectures and courses about it.
>
> To use it in your life, you need more than just to be aware of its existence. You need to adopt the attitude of positive thinking in everything you do.
>
> **With a positive attitude** we experience pleasant and happy feelings. This brings brightness to the eyes, more energy, and happiness. Our whole being broadcasts good will, happiness and success. Even our health is affected in a beneficial way. We walk tall, our voice is more powerful, and our body language shows the way we feel.   (Remez Sasson, successconsciousness.com)

6. Embrace Enthusiasm

Be the day's cheerleader.
All days are good; some are better than others.

You will find enthusiasm is contagious; give some to others.

Show off!

Tell people how happy you are to be pursuing your dream. And as you move closer to your goal, reward yourself with praise.

7. Take Action and End Procrastination

I can't say this enough: you can have the best plan in the world, but if you don't take action on it you simply have a dream. Are you self-motivated, or do you need external motivation from someone else?

Self-motivated people are rewarded by their own achievements. Of course, all of us are pleased with ourselves for meeting goals. Some of us, though, are more motivated by positive feedback from others. This feedback may come in different forms.

If your goal is financial, you may have friendly competitions with co-workers to see who gets the most contracts every week. If your goal is to be a poet, you may want to join a writers' group.

You will find feedback and encouragement that will help you stay focused on your daily goals. Determine which method of motivation works for you.

8. Take Personal Responsibility

You own this dream and you own your future. Of course, there may be setbacks and unforeseen circumstances, but you're going to treat those as opportunities, right?

It's easy to name all the things that rendered you incapable of reaching your goal, but it's a good deal more gratifying to tell how the same things didn't stop you, to describe the brilliance with which you met each challenge, or to explain how you were inspired to succeed.

Successful people don't place blame or make excuses because they don't have to. Neither do you. There is almost nothing you can't plow through or work around.

9. Learn From Your Mistakes

Everyone makes mistakes. Successful people learn extremely valuable life lessons from their mistakes. Don't be ashamed of your blunders and, more importantly, don't be afraid to make more.

Imagine what the world would be like if scientists of the past, for example, had failed to act for fear of making mistakes. Albert Einstein said, "The only sure way to avoid making mistakes is to have no new ideas."

So, envision your dream, determine what you will need to do to make it happen and then do it. Remember that the things that slow us down can actually be used as stepping stones to greater successes.

If you'll view the temporary setbacks as learning tools rather than negative life events, you are in a much better place to view the challenges with expectancy.

- ✓ Identify what's holding you back.
- ✓ Then identify what you need to do to break through to success.

This is your life – your goals – and your success.

www.ingramcontent.com/pod-product-compliance
Lightning Source LLC
Chambersburg PA
CBHW050028230526
45470CB00003B/1177